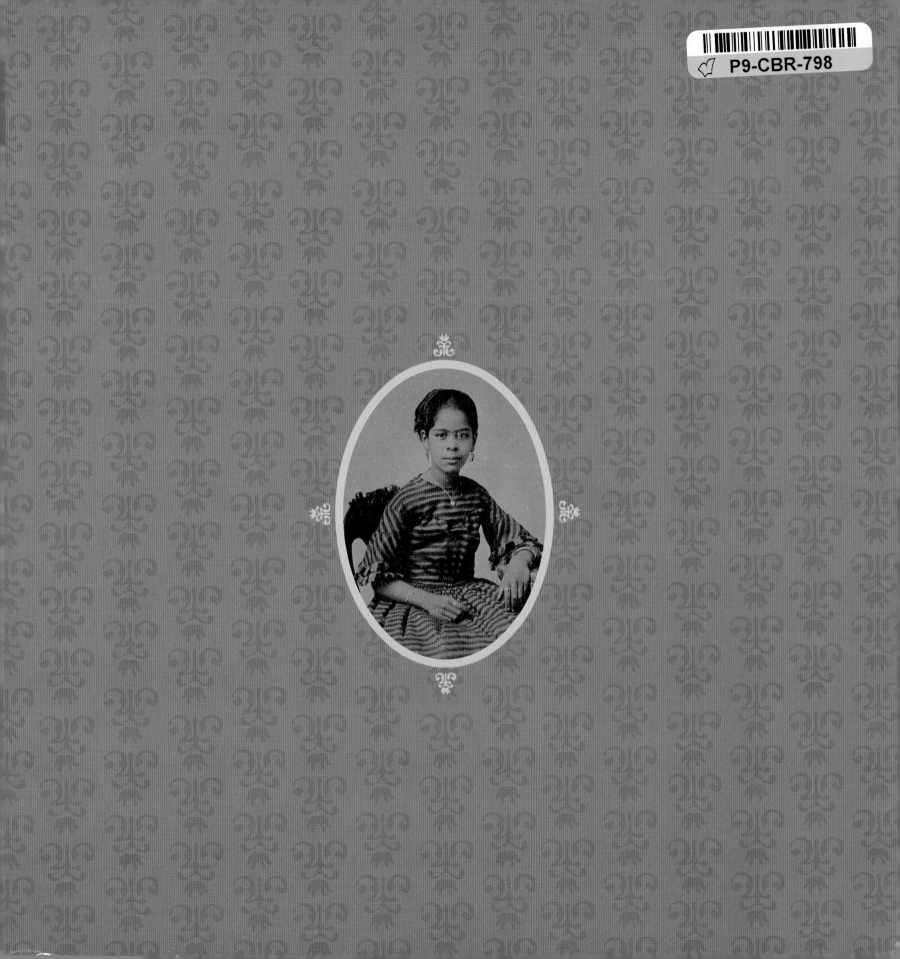

Some of the places important to Maritcha and her family are shown here. Unless stated otherwise, all the locales are in New York (modern-day Manhattan). Downtown New York is shown in further detail. From *New York and Brooklyn Map*, published 1866, by A. J. Johnson, New York.

1. 330 Pearl Street
2. 20 Vandewater Street
3. Five Points
4. 85 Centre Street, St. Philip's Protestant Episcopal Church
5. 144 Centre Street

See back of book for a map of Maritcha's journey to Rhode Island.

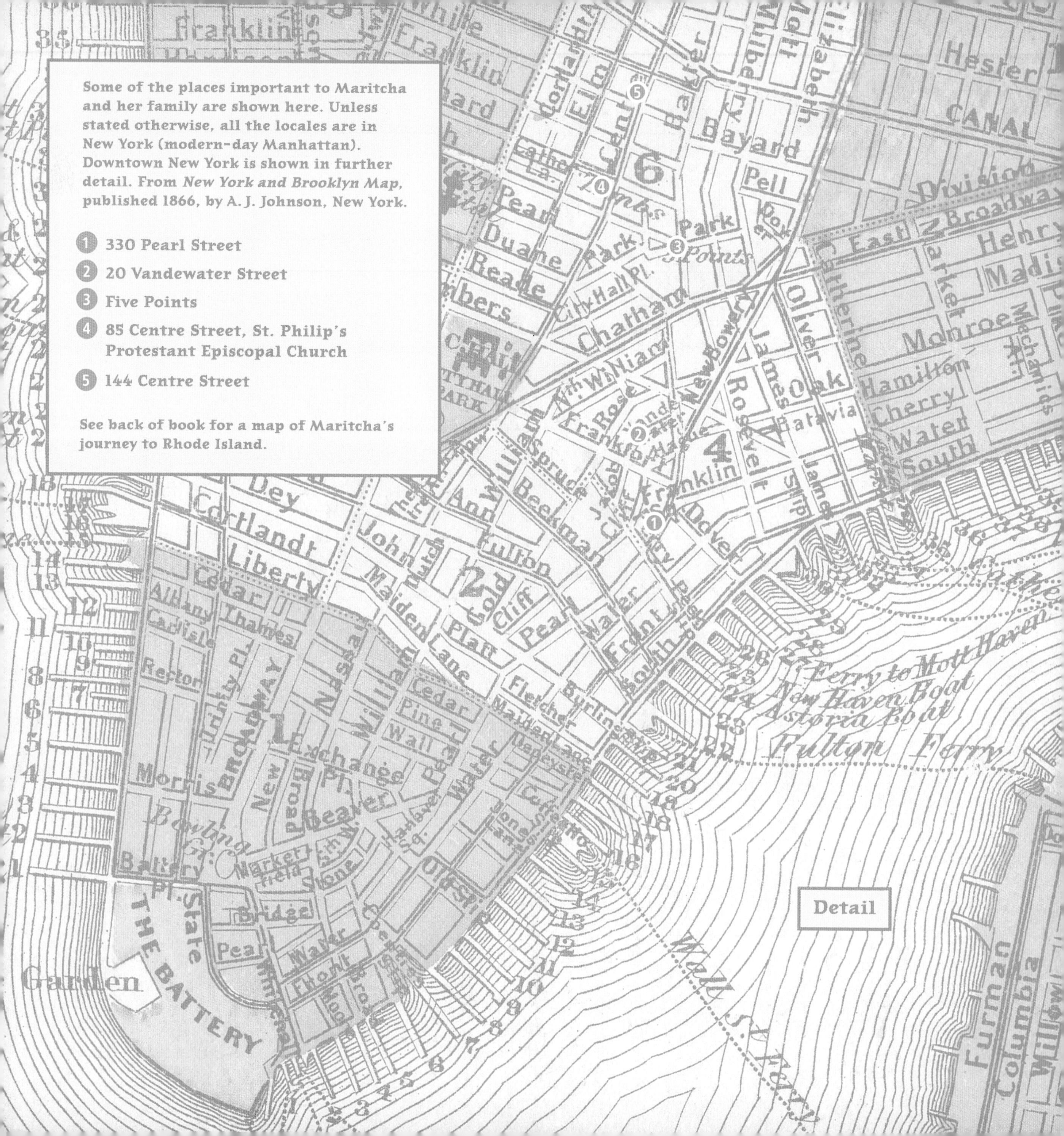

Detail

6 Elysian Fields, Hoboken, New Jersey

7 Central Park (Seneca Village occupied the area that today would have been 82nd to 89th Streets between Seventh and Eighth Avenues.)

8 Crystal Palace

9 Manhattan Colored School No. 3

10 Williamsburg, Brooklyn

Area of Detail

Maritcha

A Nineteenth-Century American Girl

Tonya Bolden

Abrams Books for Young Readers
New York

MEMORIES   OF   YESTERDAYS

All of Which I Saw and Part of Which I Was

An Autobiography

by

Maritcha Remond Lyons
Asistant Principal (retired)
Public School No. 83
Brooklyn, N. Y.

Preface

Xs blot out some words. Information gaps and blanks bewilder. Patches of faint typescript and streaky, spotted pages (microfilm printout) strain the eye. But I was too intrigued to stop reading Maritcha Rémond Lyons's memoir, *Memories of Yesterdays: All of Which I Saw and Part of Which I Was*.

Maritcha saw her memoir as "an expression of the very tender regard in which I hold my father." Her father, Albro Lyons, had often urged, "I want you to write a book; I tried to do this myself but never got further than the selection of a title—*The Gentleman in Black*." In honoring her father's wishes, Maritcha rummaged through decades of memories and keepsakes. She sorted through "the vast output of fugitive scraps [of family history] that have been gathering for years."

After I finished Maritcha's memoir, I dreamed of telling her story. Doing so would require a fair amount of detective work—dots to connect, facts to ferret out—because the memoir she never lived to revise and complete is the main source of information about her. But the challenge seemed absolutely worthwhile because Maritcha merits remembrance. Born free in a nation stained by slavery, where free blacks had few rights and rare respect, here was a girl determined to rise, to amount to something, determined to overcome.

Opposite page: Cover page of Maritcha Rémond Lyons's memoir, dated 1928, the year before she died.

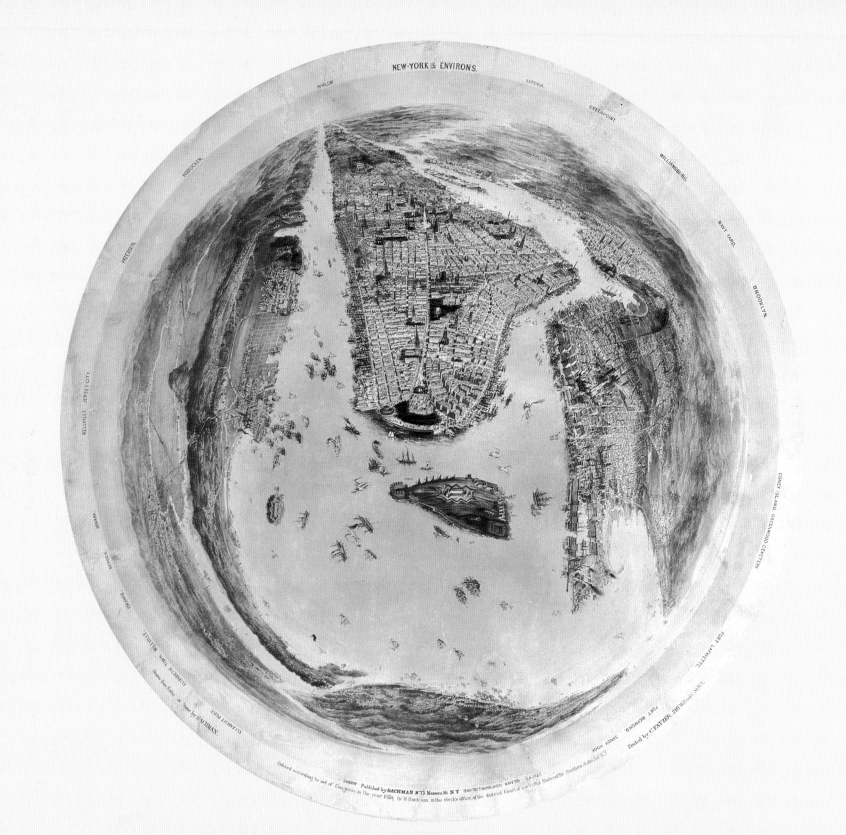

By the mid-nineteenth century, New York City was America's financial, publishing, entertainment, and manufacturing capital—and a major port—prompting one artist, in 1859, to picture the city as the center of the world.

Aim high! Stand tall! Be strong!—and *do!* These ideals were sown in the soul of young Maritcha Rémond Lyons, a child of New York City's striving class of blacks in the mid-1800s. These people "had ambitions for their offspring, took ventures, made sacrifices, much after the fashion of other Americans," Maritcha remembered. Not all of them, commonly called "colored" at the time, had suffered enslavement. Slavery, never as thick in the North as in the South, had ended in New York State in 1827.

Above: This photograph of Maritcha was taken around 1860.

Maritcha's first home was in Five Points, so-called because of a five-cornered intersection of three streets in the neighborhood: Anthony (now Worth Street), Cross (now Park Street), and Orange (now Baxter Street).

Maritcha was born some twenty years later, on May 23, 1848. At the time, the black community was tiny—less than three percent of New York City's roughly half-million residents. New York City was tiny too—just Manhattan. But even back then, it was a hustle-bustle, high-strung place of extremes: shack-and-rags poverty amid colossal wealth; virulent vice (gambling, drunkenness, brawls) alongside virtuous living.

Like many black New Yorkers, Maritcha lived in lower Manhattan. Her first home was at 144 Centre Street in the mostly black and Irish neighborhood of Five Points, a crime-ridden slum by the time Maritcha was born. She was not her parents' first or only child. There was a girl, born in 1843, who died before age three. Then, a year before Maritcha, came Therese. When Maritcha was two, she got a little sister—Pauline—and a few years later, a little brother—Albro Jr. By the time Maritcha was about eight, the Lyons family was living in and running a boardinghouse that catered to sailors at 20 Vandewater Street, a large brick house about four blocks from the East River.

If Maritcha kept a diary, it has yet to surface. One can only wonder about her day-to-day activities—and spats with sisters Therese and Pauline. There is no indication that the Lyons family had servants, so it is likely that Maritcha was helping with housekeeping by the time she was six or seven. Her chores may have included sweeping floors, featherdusting furniture, washing clothes on a washboard in a tin

SAILORS' HOME,

UNDER THE DIRECTION OF THE
AMERICAN SEAMENS' FRIEND SOCIETY,
KEPT BY
Wᴹ. P. POWELL
Nᵒ 330 Pearl St New-York City.

The logo of the boardinghouse on Pearl Street, catering to black sailors, established by the shipsmith and abolitionist William Powell. Before Maritcha was born, her father became Powell's partner. When Maritcha was about one, her father bought out Powell, and the Lyons family moved to 330 Pearl Street. The Lyons home and boardinghouse moved to 64 Oliver Street in 1853, then to 20 Vandewater Street in 1856.

tub, and ironing with a five-pound or even heavier flatiron heated on a wood- or coal-fueled cast-iron cookstove. On and in this stove, too, she probably learned to bake pies and cakes and make popular dishes of the day, from chestnut stuffing for roast turkey to oyster stew. Like other girls, Maritcha and her sisters would have spent some of their time with their "workboxes," practicing and perfecting embroidery and other needlecraft.

As for play, make-believe games with dolls, a spinning top, ring toss, and making a clackety-clack dance with a Limber Jack may have ranked high among Maritcha's delights. Leap frog, jump rope, hopscotch, hide-and-seek, and hoop and stick could have been among the fair-weather pleasures she enjoyed out on her block or in her own backyard. Evening pastimes? Checkers, or jackstraws (pick-up sticks), and possibly conjuring up rabbits, birds, and craggy faces in hand-shadows shows. Mrs. Lyons was a source of some of the laughter that laced Maritcha's life. "Mother, naturally fluent and endowed with a sense of humor was an accomplished [storyteller]; she amused us and others with gossipy, good-natured chat and was welcomed everywhere for [her] pleasant manner and her cheerful voice . . . echoing peace and goodwill."

Along with store-bought, mass-produced dolls of wax or porcelain, Maritcha may have also played with homemade cloth dolls like this one, named "Diana," which was made for a nineteenth-century American girl by her aunt.

Maritcha's parents were very social and would have attended parties similar to the one captured in this painting.

Maritcha's father, Albro Lyons, Sr., born February 10, 1814, was one of eleven children born to George Lyons, II, and Lucinda Lewis. Although born in Fishkill-on-the-Hudson in Dutchess County, New York, for most of his childhood Maritcha's father lived in New York City, on Rose Street. He attended the first African Free School in Manhattan (on William Street at the time he attended). In his youth, Albro Lyons worked at a cigar factory, then at an ice-cream company. He later became a sailor, then a porter. When he and Maritcha's mother married in May 1840, the couple started their life together in her mother's house on Centre Street.

Maritcha's younger sister, born November 12, 1850, and known as Pauline to family and friends, was baptized Mary Elizabeth Pauline Lyons. According to a relative, of all the Lyons children Pauline was "the most jovial." The Lyons family archives contain no photograph of Maritcha's older sister, Therese, born March 2, 1847.

Maritcha's mother, Mary Joseph Marshall Lyons, born July 26, 1814, spent much of her childhood in a house on Orange Street (now Baxter). She was one of three daughters born to Joseph Marshall (a house painter who hailed from Venezuela) and Elizabeth Hewlett Marshall. After her husband's death, Maritcha's grandmother opened a bakery in the basement of 144 Centre Street, a house Mr. Marshall had built.

As a young woman, Mary Marshall studied hairdressing with a French hairdresser named Martel. For a time, she worked as a clerk in the confectionary store that John and Nancy Rémond operated summers in the resort town of Newport, Rhode Island, where they also had a catering business. During the off-season, Maritcha's mother taught the Rémond daughters "various branches of hair work." One of them served as her bridesmaid, and was the person after whom young Maritcha was named.

Maritcha's little brother, Albro Lyons, Jr., born July 18, 1853.

Along with chores and family time at home, there were excursions farther afield. Maritcha recalled day trips across the Hudson River to the Elysian Fields in Hoboken, New Jersey, where people took in baseball games, had picnics, and revelled in other fresh-air activities. Another red-letter day was when her mother took her and her siblings to Manhattan's Crystal Palace, home of the "Exhibition of the Industry of All Nations"—America's first world's fair.

One of Maritcha's cherished childhood memories was of going to the Elysian Fields, site of America's first official baseball game (1846), in which the New York Nine beat the Knickerbockers twenty-three to one in four innings.

THE NEW YORK CRYSTAL PALACE.

The Crystal Palace, built to house America's first world's fair, was on Sixth Avenue between Fortieth and Forty-second Streets. North of the palace stood the 350-foot-tall Latting Observatory (at far left). The Crystal Palace opened mid-July 1853. After the world's fair closed in November 1854, the Crystal Palace was sometimes rented out for concerts and other special events. In early October 1858, a fire in a storage room flamed out of control. The cast-iron and glass palace, once hailed as fireproof, burned to the ground in less than thirty minutes.

During the world's fair, Maritcha and her family were among the crowds of New Yorkers and tourists—sometimes thousands a day—who marveled at the Crystal Palace's display of astonishments—from ancient armor from the Tower of London and fancy French china, to loomed luxuries from Kashmir. During this same world's fair, Elisha Graves Otis demonstrated, in the Latting Observatory, his safety brake, which made passenger elevators (and therefore skyscrapers) more viable.

There was also the late-summer evening in 1858 when Mr. Lyons treated ten-year-old Maritcha and eleven-year-old Therese to the fireworks display at City Hall Park. The festivities celebrated the laying of about two thousand miles of cable across the Atlantic Ocean. This cable enabled Europe and America to engage in the most advanced form of communication at the time: telegraphy. (But the cable failed in early September 1858, and was not operational until the mid-1860s.)

During fireside family time on chilly autumn evenings or thunderstorm afternoons—that's when Maritcha's mother's mother, Elizabeth Hewlett Marshall, who lived with the family until her death in 1861, may have satisfied Maritcha's curiosity about New York City before she was born. Grandmother Marshall remembered winters as "continuously severe," with the city sometimes snow-logged from November to late April and the East River so "regularly frozen over" that "walking across it [was] among one of the winter recreations." Maritcha's father "recollected seeing a barbecue on the ice in celebration of Washington's birthday."

Maritcha squirreled away family history. One bittersweet nugget was that Grandfather Marshall, as well as her father, had owned property far uptown in Seneca Village, a largely black hamlet, with some Irish, German, and Native American residents. By the early 1850s, Seneca Village, with its school and three churches, was aiming to build up into a more stable, hearty community. That hope died a few years later when city officials decided that Seneca Village and other communities had to go. They were in the way of plans for what one man called "nineteenth-century America's greatest work of art": the 800-plus-acre Central Park.

Maritcha took pride, however, in knowing that Grandfather Marshall and Grandfather Lyons had a hand in the renovation of St. Philip's Protestant Episcopal Church's first home on Collect Street (Centre Street's original name). Maritcha's parents had been married at St. Philip's, the church Maritcha attended for much of her childhood. Maritcha knew that, like many early black churches in America, the founding of St. Philip's sprang from protest. Black parishioners of the city's oldest Episcopal church, Trinity, grew weary of segregated seating. (Typically, blacks attending white-run churches had to sit in the back pews or the balcony.)

Maritcha's family attended St. Philip's Church in New York City. Created around the same time as Maritcha's childhood, this illustration pictures a congregation in Washington, D.C., and shows how she and her family may have dressed to attend services and other church functions.

One family member Maritcha learned little about was Grandmother Marshall's brother, James Hewlett—an outcast, because of the rather unsavory life he lived. Though shunned by some family members, Maritcha's great-uncle received audiences' applause as a star at the African Grove Theatre in New York City and performed on other stages elsewhere in the nation as well as in England and Trinidad.

In contrast to her great-uncle, the abolitionist Frederick Douglass had to have been a close-to-holy topic of conversation. When Maritcha was a child, Frederick Douglass was the most famous black person in the world. Maritcha treasured her grandmother's memory of the day a family friend, Charles Rémond, brought Douglass to the Centre

Top: Marticha's great-uncle, James Hewlett (c.1780–c.1850) was a ship's steward before he became an actor, a profession many people regarded as not very respectable. After the African Grove Theatre closed in the mid-1820s, Hewlett often presented selections from William Shakespeare's play *Richard III* (his favorite role) in his one-man shows. Hewlett's offstage antics included petty larceny, another reason Maritcha's family wanted nothing to do with him.

Bottom: Frederick Douglass (c. 1818–1895) escaped slavery in Maryland in 1838 by passing himself off as a free sailor. By the time Maritcha was born, Douglass was one of the most prominent antislavery activists: giving stirring speeches around the nation, and writing poignant articles for various periodicals, most especially for the weekly newspaper he cofounded in 1847, *The North Star* (later, *Frederick Douglass's Paper*, after it merged with another paper).

Street house. After Douglass recounted the story of his bondage and daring escape to freedom, Grandmother Marshall wished him strength in his anti-slavery work. She pledged that whenever he came to town, "you will find a seat at my table, a place to sleep and I will keep your linen laundered for you."

While Maritcha enjoyed many buoyant, glorious days, her life was not carefree. At one point, illness struck. She never named her disability, but her treatment involved wearing "mechanical appliances . . . for the support of my spine for the improvement of my carriage." She may have suffered from scoliosis, a curvature of the spine. Fortunately, Maritcha's health was in the hands of an excellent doctor, James McCune Smith, her parents' childhood friend, best man at their wedding, and godfather to all their children. One of the things Maritcha's parents did to keep her spirits up while she recovered was purchase a piano and arrange for piano lessons.

Engraved by Patrick H.Reason.

Maritcha's godfather, Dr. James McCune Smith (1813–1865), a leading antislavery activist, was born in New York City, where he graduated from African Free School No. 2 (Mulberry Street), with honors. In 1832, after American colleges had denied him admission because he was black, Smith went to Scotland. There, he enrolled in the University of Glasgow. In five years he earned his bachelor's, master's, and medical degrees. When he returned to New York City, Dr. Smith started what would become a successful interracial medical practice at 55 West Broadway, where he also ran a pharmacy.

By spring 1861, thirteen-year-old Maritcha was back on her feet and longing to return to school. Though her spelling, reading, and "ciphering," as arithmetic was called, had not been "allowed to rust from disuse," Maritcha was behind. "I could neither write my name legibly nor do a sum in long division." She desperately wanted to catch up, and did so at Manhattan's Colored School No. 3, uptown, on Broadway and Thirty-seventh Street. The school's principal, Charles Reason, was a friend of her parents. Under his supervision, Maritcha plunged into a remedial program—"I had arithmetic and grammar exclusively." At home, she was tutored in geography and history. In time, she entered the regular

Maritcha may have spent some of her school days in a classroom like this one.

Busy, bustling Broadway—a street Maritcha was familiar with, especially on the days she had to walk to school.

course of study. Maritcha remembered Principal Reason as being "quite intolerant of mediocrity." His zeal for excellence was contagious, quickening in her a "love of study for study's sake."

While Maritcha loved school, the journey to and fro was fraught with some anxiety. She never knew whether a stagecoach would stop for her or not. "Once in awhile one would respond to my signal, but oftener I was ignored or jeered at." So "oftener" Maritcha walked the roughly three miles, and "as the exercise did no apparent harm, I was enabled to endure to the end."

What enabled Maritcha to endure whatever the weather? True grit. And she had plenty of examples around her. Her godfather had gone all the way to Scotland to pursue his dream of becoming a doctor and then inspired others to high ideals and achievement. At his pharmacy in lower Manhattan, Dr. Smith dispensed more than pills and potions. Maritcha remembered the pharmacy's back room, with its library, as a "rallying" center, where people gathered for "discussions and debates on all the topics of the day." These would have ranged from the abolition of slavery to segregated schooling to the fact that, unlike white men, black men could vote in local elections only if they owned real estate worth at least two hundred and fifty dollars, about half a year's wage for many people. (Women could not vote at all.)

Maritcha also looked up to the wealthy Thomas Downing, a constant, generous contributor to black schools and self-help organizations. This freeborn Virginian had risen from an oyster harvester and vendor to owner of a thriving catering business and restaurant, the Oyster House. Downing's restaurant, on Broad Street, close by Wall Street, was extremely popular with the city's white elite—bankers, merchants, stockbrokers, politicians—few if any of whom knew that the Oyster House cellar sometimes served as a hiding place for people who had escaped from slavery in Maryland, Virginia, and elsewhere in the South.

More than Dr. Smith, more than Thomas Downing—Maritcha admired no one more than her parents. She credited them with transforming a "sickly, peevish, unproposing girl" into someone ready "to do the best for myself with the view of making the best of myself." By word and deed, her parents, like their friends, signaled that this best self should not be selfish and self-absorbed, but of service to others.

Maritcha's father was a member of do-good organizations throughout his life. One was the New York African Society for Mutual Relief, something of an unemployment and life insurance provider and Salvation Army rolled into one. "At anti-slavery meetings and conferences, mother was almost invariably present," Maritcha remembered, "not to agitate but to learn her duty." This "duty" was

Beginning in the 1830s, Maritcha's father was a delegate to several black conventions. At these gatherings people talked about the needs of their communities and ways of improving their people's lives. The convention pictured here was held in Washington, D.C.

being an ace operator for the Underground Railroad, the secret network of people who helped streams of youngsters and adults escape from slavery and start new lives.

As a boardinghouse, the Lyons's home made an ideal safe house for escaped slaves. The sight of different people coming and going from 20 Vandewater Street would hardly arouse suspicion. So Maritcha grew up glimpsing "many strange faces" in her home. "Under mother's vigilant eye, refugees were kept long enough to be fed and to have disguises changed and be met by those prepared to speed them on in the journey toward the North Star," that is, farther north—even all the way to Canada, where slavery had been outlawed. Maritcha's father estimated that he and his wife helped about a thousand people. "So alert and faithful were my parents to their 'traveling brethren,' that no emergency found them unprepared. . . . They were only samples of the great majority of our people in the free states who worked, suffered, and prayed that no one who had the courage to start on the untoward venture should fail to reach the goal."

Many of the escaped slaves that Maritcha's parents and their friends helped would have begun their journey at night, following the "Drinking Gourd," as the Big Dipper was called, because it points the way to the North Star.

Maritcha knew never to breathe a word about her parents' Underground Railroad work—"Children were taught then to neither see, hear, nor talk about the affairs in which grown-ups were concerned." Her parents could be fined and imprisoned if authorities discovered that they were helping runaway slaves. All the while that Maritcha kept hush-hush about her parents' heroism, she never imagined that one day she would be on the run and a refugee. This happened amid the catastrophe that hit New York City shortly after Maritcha turned fifteen, during the sweltering days of mid-July 1863.

A look down Maritcha's block, at the corner of Frankfort and Vandewater Streets, in 1863.

By the summer of 1863, the Civil War was in its second year. With fewer men volunteering for military service, the Union had decided to start drafting able-bodied white men ages twenty to forty-five. (Blacks who wanted to serve as soldiers in the Union Army were not yet being accepted.)

The draft was extremely unpopular, especially among low-wage workers. For the rich, there was a loophole: if drafted, a man could buy an exemption for three hundred dollars. This infuriated the poorer population. Too, many white New Yorkers, poor to wealthy, had come to hate the war because they felt it was less about keeping the North and the South one nation and more about ending slavery. And many of them had no quarrel with slavery. Many had grown rich from doing business with slaveholders—buying their raw materials, reaped from slave labor, for manufacture of goods; selling them luxury items; and making money from loans to them. Poor whites saw abolition as a threat to their live-lihoods: more free blacks would mean stiffer competition for jobs.

New York City's draft began on Saturday, July 11, 1863. The names of more than one thousand draftees appeared in the newspapers the next day. That weekend there was great griping and grumbling on street corners and stoops, in beer halls and saloons. Some prepared to protest come Monday when more draftees would be announced at the draft office uptown on Third Avenue.

Early Monday morning, word spread that waves of white men in lower Manhattan—ironworkers, dock workers, construction workers—had gone on strike. Banging pots as they trooped up to Central Park for a no-draft rally, the strikers roused others—stonemasons, carpenters, cartmen—to walk off their jobs. A march on the draft office followed the rally and before long—mayhem!

Telegraph poles—hacked down! Rail tracks—yanked up! Wooden fences—ripped apart! With planks, crowbars, bricks, broadaxes, knives, and guns, a whirlwind of mobs went wild. The rioters, immigrants and natives, were of various white ethnicities, with the majority Irish, then the most downtrodden white New

The draft lottery at the provost marshal's office on Third Avenue between Forty-sixth and Forty-seventh streets started at 10:30 A.M. on Monday July 13, 1863. After several dozen names were pulled, members of a volunteer firefighting company, incensed that they were not exempt from the draft, stormed the place and set it on fire. The fire spread to neighboring stores and a tenement building.

Yorkers. At the same time, many of the firefighters and police officers who tried to quell the chaos were also Irish. Whatever their ethnicity, the rioters had common targets: pro-war politicians and other government officials, rich people, abolitionists, and blacks of all classes. During four days of savage rage, mobs

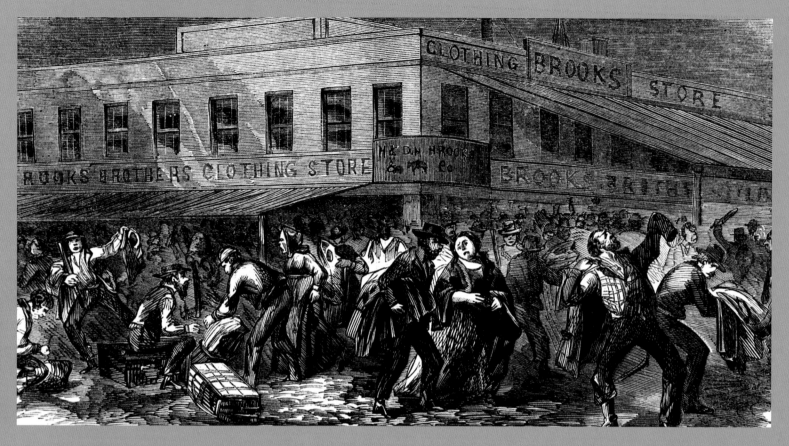

Above: The upscale clothing store Brooks Brothers, on Catherine and Cherry streets, was among the scores of stores looted during what the *New York Times* called, "The Reign of the Rabble." Below: During the riots, some people escaped the clutches of the mobs that roamed the city streets. Those who did not were badly beaten—or worse, killed.

assaulted draft officials and police officers. They attacked mansions on Fifth Avenue and elegant town houses elsewhere in the city. They dragged blacks from streetcars, chased them down broad avenues and skinny cobble-stone streets, and cornered them in alleys. One mob torched and looted the orphanage for black children where Maritcha's godfather served as head physician.

Maritcha's home came under assault around 6:30 P.M. on the second day of the riots, with "a rabble . . . breaking window panes, smashing shutters, and partially demolishing the main front door." Fortunately, something drew the mob's attention away from her home. Maritcha's parents barricaded their front door, using stones the mob had hurled at their home. According to a *New York Times* article, "nine of the inmates were injured." Presumably, these were boarders. Maritcha made no mention that her parents were hurt during the attack—nor of her and her siblings' whereabouts at the time. She only indicated that "before dusk" they were in a far safer place, quite possibly in Williamsburg, across the East River.

The *New York Times* article that reported on the first attack on Maritcha's home.

That night, Maritcha's parents sat on guard in their front hall, "determined to protect their property. . . . Lights having been extinguished, a lonely vigil of hours passed in mingled darkness, indignation, uncertainty, and dread. Just after midnight, a yell announced that a second mob was gathering to attempt assault." Footfalls up the front steps of 20 Vandewater Street followed the yell. Before troublemakers could close in, Maritcha's father "advanced into the doorway and fired point blank into the crowd." That single shot sufficed to scare the rabble off. Maritcha's father was no doubt trigger-ready when around dawn he again heard footsteps nearing his home.

"Don't shoot, Al. It's only me." The speaker was a police officer named Kelly. "This kind-hearted man sat on our steps and sobbed like a child." Officer Kelly lamented that when he heard about the attack, he had been unable to send help—and help was what Maritcha's parents needed the next day when another mob mounted an attack—this one fiercer—sending them to flight.

Maritcha's father hopped the back fence and raced to a nearby police station on Oak Street, "pursued through the streets by a howling mob," a newspaper later reported. Maritcha's mother fled to the home of their German next-door neighbor. Earlier that day, he had loosened boards in the fence between their homes "in anticipation of an emergency." Several weeks later, the man was "waylaid." He was one of many whites assaulted during and after the riots for having come to a black person's aid.

During the third attack, rioters ran amok in Maritcha's home for about an hour, until the police arrived on the scene: "What a home! Its interior was dismantled, furniture was missing or broken. From basement to attic evidences of the worst vandalism prevailed. A fire, kindled in one of the upper rooms, was discovered in time to prevent a conflagration." Maritcha's parents knew it would be foolhardy to remain in their home another night. Like droves of other New Yorkers, they took refuge in a police station. After nightfall, police officers escorted Maritcha's parents to the East River to catch a steamboat to

The police alone could not stop the rioting. By late Thursday, July 16, 1863, more than five thousand Union troops had been sent to the city's rescue.

Williamsburg. After collecting their children, Mrs. Lyons took them farther out of harm's way, while Mr. Lyons secured their home and salvaged whatever he could.

Maritcha's father left a record of the cost of restoring their home, from repairing the front door, putting in new windows, and plastering and painting, to replacing the family's possessions. His list of "property destroyed or stolen by a riotous mob" began with "1 English Rug" and included a divan, four mahogany chairs, a gilt-framed "Looking Glass," a pair of French mantel vases, nine Brittania lamps, an oil painting, a bronze eight-day clock, "1 Spy Glass," "1 Set Chessmen," thirty-five grass pillows, blankets, tablecloths, towels, a reading-room table, a piano and piano stool, two and a half dozen cups and saucers, three dozen breakfast plates, a dinner bell, frying pans, iron stew pans, copper kettles, pudding dishes, "Washtubs and boards," eight pounds of Castile soap, a coal scuttle, a barrel of brown sugar, as well as coffee, tea, flour, rice, potatoes, hominy, and cornmeal.

This inventory, more than a dozen pages long, lists each family member's lost belongings. Along with clothing, Therese's included a silk umbrella, a writing desk, and a pair of skates; Pauline's, a pair of Balmoral shoes (lace-up ankle boots), a hoop skirt, three cotton flannel skirts, three calico dresses, and a large doll. A pair of boots, four pairs of Nankeen pants, four calico shirts, a sled, and an American flag were among ten-year-old Albro Jr.'s losses. The mob stole or ruined Maritcha's poplin, organdie, and French calico dresses; six muslin skirts, a pair

Page one of the damages to their home and the losses Maritcha and her family suffered during the riots. Maritcha's father misdated the inventory July 12; the riots did not begin until the following day.

of kid gloves; and her workbox, among other things. When Maritcha's father tallied everything up, it came to about two thousand dollars, equivalent to roughly thirty-five thousand dollars today.

What will become of us now? Will we ever return home? Will father be safe? Questions like these no doubt hounded Maritcha as she, Therese, Pauline, Albro Jr., and their mother made the roughly one-hundred-mile journey to the end of Long Island (possibly via the Long Island Rail Road), where they boarded a boat bound for the small whaling town of New London, Connecticut. There, they rested in the home of friends, the Andersons, before

Maritcha and her family would have boarded a train similar to this one at the start of their journey, which would end in Salem, Massachusetts.

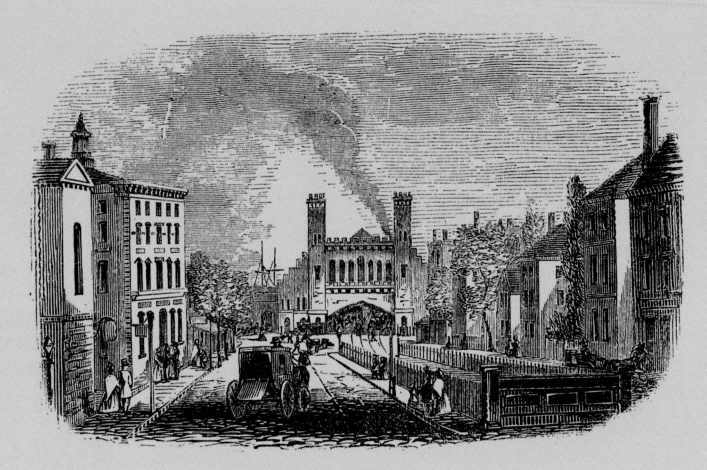

**A street scene of Salem, Massachusetts, where Maritcha's
family took refuge after the Draft Riots.**

heading farther north to Salem, Massachusetts. Salem was the home of long-time friends, the Rémonds, a family of entrepreneurs and antislavery activists.

Reaching Salem probably meant taking a railroad ferry from New London to Groton, followed by an overland rail ride to Boston, and then a horse-drawn carriage or another train ride to their final destination—"We reached Salem tired, travel stained," Maritcha remembered, "with only the garments we had on." She never forgot how the Rémond family "outdid themselves in showering upon us kind attentions, anxious to cheer and to incite hope to replace despair."

By late fall 1863, Maritcha's father had made 20 Vandewater Street livable. Back together again in New York, the Lyons family did their best to resume normal lives. For Maritcha, that included returning to Colored School No. 3, and graduating in the spring of 1864. By then, she knew New York would not be home for much longer. Following what became known as the New York City Draft Riots, the worst of all the draft riots during the summer of 1863 and the worst riot the country had ever seen, thousands of blacks quit New York City. Some moved across the river to the city of Brooklyn; others, even farther away. The small shipping, cotton-mill, and manufacturing town of Providence, Rhode Island, became Maritcha's new home.

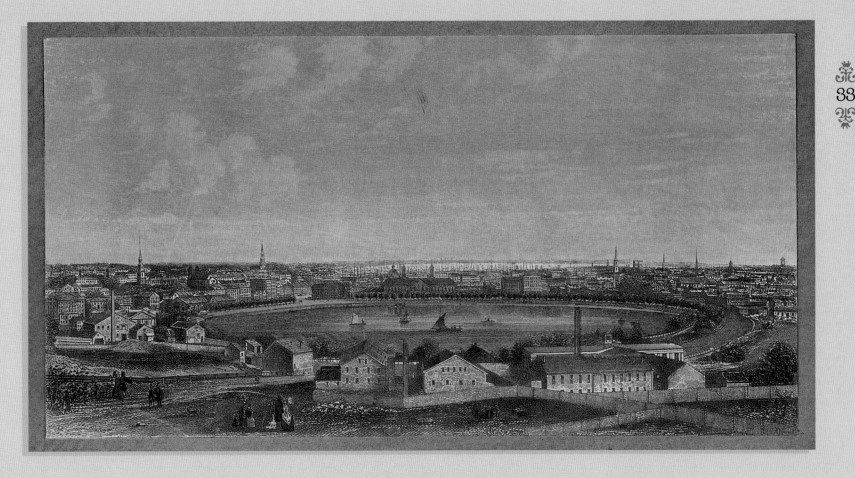

A mid-nineteenth-century bird's-eye view of Providence, Rhode Island, where Maritcha made history.

Maritcha's father drew on his early work experience at an ice-cream company to support his family in their new home.

Maritcha and her family eventually settled in a house at 16 B Street. As before, home was also a place of business. Her father opened an ice-cream shop and catering business. Her mother became a hairdresser again. A place to live and a livelihood were not their only concerns. Maritcha's parents wanted her, Pauline, and Albro Jr. to continue their education. (Therese, finished with school, was on her way to becoming a skilled seamstress.)

Pauline and Albro Jr. were enrolled in a grammar school for blacks. But Maritcha had nowhere to go because there was no high school for blacks. When her mother tried to enroll her in the Girls' Department of Providence High, school officials would not allow it. Maritcha and her parents refused to take no for an answer. Foremost among their supporters was a former New Yorker: George Downing, son of Thomas Downing of Oyster House fame. George Downing, who at one point had a catering business in Providence and a resort hotel in Newport, Rhode Island, had launched a campaign against segregated schooling in that state before Maritcha and her family moved to Providence.

Maritcha's case landed in the hands of the Rhode Island state legislature. She was even required to speak before this powerful body of lawmakers. "I, but sixteen years old, made my maiden speech and, in a trembling voice, pleaded for the opening of the door of opportunity." Maritcha won!

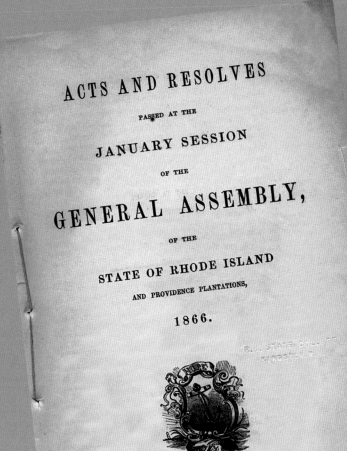

ACTS AND RESOLVES

PASSED AT THE

JANUARY SESSION

OF THE

GENERAL ASSEMBLY,

OF THE

STATE OF RHODE ISLAND

AND PROVIDENCE PLANTATIONS,

1866.

PROVIDENCE:
PROVIDENCE PRESS COMPANY, PRINTERS TO THE STATE.
1866.

JANUARY, 1866.

CHAPTER 609.

AN ACT IN ADDITION TO TITLE XIII OF THE REVISED STATUTES, "OF PUBLIC INSTRUCTION."

It is enacted by the General Assembly as follows:

SECTION 1. In deciding upon applications for admission to any school in this State, maintained wholly or in part at the public expense, no distinction shall be made on account of the race or color of the applicant.

SEC. 2. This act shall take effect on the 15th day of May next.

SEC. 3. All acts or parts of acts inconsistent herewith are hereby repealed.

Maritcha's plea for the "opening of the door of opportunity" was one of a series of events that led the Rhode Island legislature to pass a law that the state's public schools could not deny a child admission "on account of the race or color of the applicant."

While the legislature ruled that Maritcha had the right to attend Providence High, the school questioned her aptitude. As Maritcha explained, "a certificate of graduation from Colored Grammar School 3, New York City, would not be accepted as qualifying for admission." Maritcha was "forced to take an examination, and to do this I had to enter a grammar school which I did five weeks previous to the semi-annual examination for promotion from elementary to high school." A "grilling examination, written and oral," is how Maritcha described that test—which she passed.

During her first year of high school (1865-1866), Maritcha sat alone at a double desk. There was an overflow of students that year, but her classmates preferred to sit "in window seats or on the corners of the platform" rather than sit beside her. Maritcha stayed focused on the point important: to *learn*— maximize her mind, hone skills, and decide what she wanted to make of herself after graduation. The Civil War had ended in the spring of 1865. Several months later, slavery had been abolished throughout the United States. While Maritcha was in high school, the nation was in the midst of Reconstruction, with many people, in and out of government, endeavoring to make the country a more equitable and enlightened place. Many young adults, like Maritcha, were eager to do their part.

Although life at Providence High started out rough for Maritcha, things smoothed out some in time. By senior year, she was "one of the foremost of the leaders." Yet, she was "indifferent to the popularity." She was friendly toward schoolmates friendly toward her. She took part in school activities, such as playing piano for the choral club. But Maritcha kept her guard up. "The iron had entered my soul. I never forgot that I had to sue for a privilege which any but a colored girl could have without asking." Looking back on her days at Providence High, Maritcha referred to only one classmate as "my

Maritcha's high school, Providence High (on Benefit Street),
as it looked in the late nineteenth century.

Which furnishes the better subjects
for art, Mythology, or Christianity?

M. R. Lyons   May 5. 1869.

P. H. S. Girls' Department.

"We live through admiration, hope, and
love". To stimulate and strengthen these vi-
tal aspirations is the special mission of
the artist, a mission most exalted in charac-
ter, and whose influences radiate to the limits
of society. The poet, painter, or sculptor, endowed with a vivid and brilliant imagination and that profound insight into nature that men call genius, diffuses, by
various forms of art, the elements of beauty,
loveliness and grandeur which mould
the taste and sentiment of an age.

In the works of nature, the great
artist, beauty and sublimity are dis-
played in multitudinous forms for the
especial gratification of the senses, and
expansion of the intellect; yet the grand

chum." That girl, with whom she remained a lifelong friend, was Lucia Tappan, grand-niece of ardent abolitionists Arthur, Lewis, and Benjamin Tappan.

Maritcha "never had less than the highest marks," and when it came to compositions, she relished writing about "race topics," such as slavery, the Underground Railroad, the Civil War, and the Draft Riots. "As I wrote out of the fullness of my heart, [my compositions] rarely failed to create a sensation." For one teacher, Maritcha's essays rarely failed to create skepticism. "Is what you wrote really true," this teacher would ask, "or have you been letting loose your imagination?"

"The half has never been told" was Maritcha's typical terse response. Not all teachers gave Maritcha grief. Sarah Doyle, who would become one of Rhode Island's leading women's rights activists, was wonderfully encouraging. Maritcha called Doyle her "guiding star."

In May 1869, shortly before her twenty-first birthday, Maritcha, who had had so many stops and starts in her education, became the first black person to graduate from Providence High. She and her friend Lucia were among the five girls chosen to read "original essays" at graduation. With her hard-won diploma, Maritcha was eager to make her own way in the world—and in doing so, help children do the best for themselves with the view of making the best of themselves. Maritcha became a teacher, "with never a doubt as to a proper choice of a vocation."

Opposite page: The essay Maritcha read on graduation day, "Which Furnishes the Better Subjects for Art, Mythology or Christianity?" took up nine pages in a booklet of about 6 x 4 inches. Maritcha's essay concluded with the following words: "As in art so in poetry, the 'linked sweetness' of the rhythmic line should touch and inspire the heart not less than it attracts the ear and delights the taste. Imagination and the sense of beauty assume their noblest functions only when they minister at the altars of the highest good and the highest truths."

Author's Note

Several years ago, while I was researching a project at the Schomburg Center for Research in Black Culture, Diana Lachatanere, curator of its Manuscripts, Archives, and Rare Books Division, brought Maritcha's memoir to my attention. As I read the eighty-one-page typescript, I felt a kinship. Maritcha's heroes included people I count among my inspirations. And here was a girl who had spent most of her youth in Manhattan, where I spent my wonder years, specifically in Harlem, the Schomburg's home. Finding Maritcha, born over a century before me, allowed me insights into my city's history, and imaginings of what my life might have been like had I been a child when she was.

Maritcha remained, to borrow from Toni Morrison, "a friend of mind" over the years. When I began work on my book about black children in America, *Tell All the Children Our Story*, I knew Maritcha would have a presence in that book. Not long after its release, I felt ready to tackle Maritcha's story. Given the dearth of children's books about freeborn blacks in antebellum America, I believed *Maritcha* would be of interest to New Yorkers and non-New Yorkers alike.

My editor and I decided against presenting the story with illustrations by a contemporary artist because the Schomburg had photographs and other keepsakes from Maritcha's life. Not to draw on these holdings would be a missed opportunity to bring historical artifacts into wider view. To further add texture to Maritcha's story, I sought out images from other sources. In some cases, given the scarcity of

Along with being a respected educator, Maritcha Lyons was also a gifted orator, lending her voice to calls for equal opportunity for blacks and women. She did the same as a member of several civic organizations. One she cofounded was the White Rose Mission, which opened in Manhattan in the late 1890s as a "Christian, non-sectarian Home for Colored Girls and Women, where they may be trained in the principles of practical self-help and right living." The photograph on the opposite page was taken when Maritcha was teaching at Brooklyn's P.S. 83.

nonderogatory images of blacks in pre-Civil War America, I settled on images that match Maritcha's era and experiences, but are not precisely of her life and environs. Similarly, full caption credits for the artwork are given in the backmatter, not alongside the illustrations. Here, it is the picture and not the artist or medium that is essential. Another decision my editor and I made at the outset was to limit the book's focus to Maritcha's youth, a period that the book's primary readership would identify with and find most interesting.

For those curious about Maritcha's adulthood, I offer the following summary:

In October 1869, Maritcha Rémond Lyons began what would be a nearly fifty-year career as an educator. Her first teaching position was at Brooklyn's Colored School No. 1, whose principal, Charles Dorsey, was a friend of her father. For several years, on weeknights and weekends, Maritcha continued her own education through private study with more experienced teachers, and courses at local institutions. In 1898, she became an assistant principal at Brooklyn's Public School No. 83 ("colored" schools were no more). That same year, New York City (by then Manhattan and the Bronx) merged with Brooklyn, Queens, and Staten Island for the making of one city, Greater New York. Maritcha Lyons retired from teaching in 1918.

By 1928, the year she typed up the only known draft of her memoir, Maritcha Lyons was the last surviving member of her immediate family. In the late 1880s, her parents, having lived for a time in Plainfield, New Jersey, had moved into the home

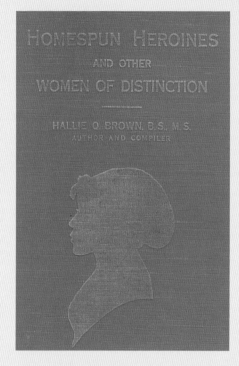

Maritcha Lyons contributed eight biographies to Hallie Q. Brown's book *Homespun Heroines and Other Women of Distinction* (1926). One of the women she profiled was the legendary Underground Railroad "conductor," Harriet Tubman. Another was Brooklyn-born Dr. Susan McKinney Steward, the third black woman in America to earn a medical degree. Dr. Steward and Maritcha Lyons were close friends.

Maritcha and Albro Jr. shared at 51 St. Felix Street in Brooklyn. (Neither Maritcha nor Albro Jr. ever married.) Maritcha's mother died in 1894; her father, two years later. Between their deaths, Maritcha lost twice-widowed Pauline, a nurse in Oakland, California. In 1906, Maritcha's brother died. At one point Albro Jr. had been a pharmacist in a drugstore near 20 Vandewater Street, owned by Philip White, a protégé of Dr. James McCune Smith.

Back in 1871, in Providence, the oldest Lyons daughter, Therese, had married a printer, Charles Burrill, with whom she had one child, George Willis Burrill. The family lived in Plainsfield, New Jersey, and then in Nashville, Tennessee, where Therese's husband worked for the National Baptist Publishing Company and cofounded *The Nashville Globe*. Therese and her family were living in Brooklyn when she died in 1924. Maritcha Lyons spent her last years in the Bayshore home of Therese's son, a former printer who worked for the Long Island Rail Road.

"I now find myself practically a 'shut-in,'" Maritcha Lyons wrote at that time. In reflecting on her adult life, one of her brightest memories was the day, while visiting Washington, D.C., she met with Frederick Douglass. "Instead of waiting to be called upon as in his high position it was the customary and courteous thing for strangers to do," she recalled, "I had the honor of being the recipient of a call from him. In brief but well chosen words he referred to the wholeheartedness of grandmother, made kind inquiries about my parents and sent to them messages of esteem and regard. This action on the part of one who had attained the pinnacle of greatness, yet who did not forget the day of small things . . . is surely worthy of permanent record."

Before Maritcha died, on January 28, 1929, at age eighty, the "fugitive scraps" of family history were in the hands of Pauline's oldest son, Henry ("Harry") Albro Williamson. This one-time chiropodist, one-time postal worker had a passion for black history, including that of his family. His archives included records and keepsakes his grandfather and aunt had preserved—including her memoir—all of which passed into the care of the Schomburg Center for Research in Black Culture.

Notes

Unless cited below, all information about Maritcha Rémond Lyons and quotations are from her memoir, *Memories of Yesterdays: All of Which I Saw and Part of Which I Was*, 1928, 81 pages. Harry A. Williamson Papers. New York: The Schomburg Center for Research in Black Culture, The New York Public Library, Astor, Lenox and Tilden Foundations. Sc Micro R-3984, Reel 1. Obvious typographical and punctuation errors have been corrected.

Page 3

Rémond. Although present-day references to the Rémond family, after whom Maritcha was named, generally do not have the accent, Maritcha did put an accent over her middle name. I have followed her lead throughout.

Page 6-7

On birth and death dates of Maritcha and her family here and throughout. "The Family of George Lyons, 1st and other genealogical records." Harry A. Williamson Papers, op. cit.

On New York City's black population in the late 1840s. According to the U.S. Census Bureau, in 1840 the city had 16,358 blacks within a total population of 312,710; in 1850, the numbers were 13,815 and 515,547, respectively. University of Virginia Geospatial and Statistical Data Center. United States Historical Census Data Browser. Online. 1998. University of Virginia. Available at: *http://fisher.lib.virginia.edu/census/*. Date last accessed October 29, 2008.

On dates of the Lyons family's residences. Record of Assessment, Manhattan, 4th Ward, 1834-1860; 1860-1876. Municipal Archives, New York City Department of Records and Information Services, 31 Chambers Street, New York, New York 10007.

Page 11

"[T]he most jovial." "The Family of George Lyons, 1st and other genealogical records." Harry A. Williamson Papers, op. cit.

Page 14-15

On Maritcha's outing to the fireworks at City Hall. She erroneously wrote that she was "eight" at the time. "[N]ineteenth-century . . . art." Unidentified man quoted in Ric Burns et al.: *New York: An Illustrated History.* (New York: Knopf, 1999), p. 113.

On St. Philip's. The church was established as St. Philip's Colored Episcopal Church in 1818, ten years after blacks attending Trinity Episcopal Church withdrew. The church, which had several homes in lower Manhattan, eventually settled in Harlem, on West 134th Street.

Page 16

On Frederick Douglass's visit to Maritcha's grandmother's house. Maritcha indicated that her parents were married at the time of the visit. They married in 1840, so the visit had to have been between 1840 and 1848. According to the chronology in *Douglass: Autobiographies* (New York: The Library of America, 1994), p. 1055, Douglass first met Charles Rémond in 1842. Douglass lectured in New York State several times during the 1840s.

Page 18

On Maritcha's schooling in New York City. Before her illness, for reasons that are not clear, Maritcha, along with Therese, attended a school across the East River in Williamsburg, Brooklyn (Williamsburgh, which became part of the city of Brooklyn in the 1850s, dropped the "h" at the end of its name, though for years some would still use "Williamsburgh"). In order to attend that school they lived in Williamsburg, presumably with family friends.

Page 24

On penalty for helping escapees from slavery. According to Section 7 of the Fugitive Slave Act of 1850, anyone who hindered the capture of a runaway slave or harbored one was "subject to a fine not exceeding one thousand dollars, and imprisonment not exceeding six months." **On black serving as soldiers in the Union Army.** Thousands of blacks served as laborers, servants, spies, and in other noncombat roles since July 1861, and by mid-1863 several Union generals had raised black volunteer regiments.

Blacks were not officially admitted into the Union Army (the United States Colored Troops) until May 1863, two months after the March 3, 1863, Conscription Act.

Page 26-27

Date and time of first attack on Maritcha's home. "The Reign of the Rabble," *New York Times*, v. 12, July 15, 1863, p. 8. **"[N]ine of the inmates were injured."** Ibid.

Page 28

"by . . . a howling mob." Unsigned. "Death of Albro Lyons," *New York Age*, January 9, 1896. Harry A. Williamson Papers, op. cit.

Page 30

Mr. Lyons's inventory. Harry A. Williamson Papers, op. cit.

Page 31-32

On the journey to New London. According to Robert A. McInnes, site administrator and archivist for the New London County Historical Society, Maritcha and her family would have taken a ferry from Sag Harbor or Greenport, "probably" aboard the *Sarah S.B. Carey*. Letter to the author, September 2003.

The Andersons. Maritcha did not provide first names but in all likelihood the family was black. The New London City Directory for 1863-64, which like most directories at the time indicated when a resident was black (in this case with "colored" after the name), lists four black Andersons. There was a Jacob Anderson (truckman) and his wife residing on Mercer Street. Also living on Mercer was a Joshua Anderson (blacksmith) and an Abram Anderson (no occupation given).

On the journey to Salem, Massachusetts. According to Robert A. McInnes, site administrator and archivist for the New London County Historical Society, based on the timetables of the period, the ride from New London to Boston took a little under four hours. Letter to the author, September 2003.

The Rémond family. John and Nancy Rémond had eight children, two of whom became leading antislavery activists: Charles Lenox Rémond and Sarah Parker Rémond. In Salem, where John Rémond waged a successful campaign for the desegregation of public schools, the family continued their enterprising ways. One daughter, Susan, ended up running the catering business, along with a restaurant. Caroline, Cecilia, and Maritcha Rémond ran a beauty parlor (Ladies Hair Work Salon) and wig factory, and did brisk business with a hair tonic they made.

Page 36

"[A] certificate of graduation . . . for admission." Maritcha Lyons, "Elizabeth N. Smith" in Hallie Q. Brown, ed. *Homespun Heroines and Other Women of Distinction* (1926). Reprint with an Introduction by Randall K. Burkett, part of The Schomburg Library of Nineteenth-Century Black Women Writers. (New York: Oxford University Press, 1988), p. 20. **"[G]rilling . . . written and oral."** Maritcha Lyons, ibid., p. 20.

Page 39

Sarah Doyle. Once a student at Providence High, Sarah Elizabeth Doyle (1830-1922) began teaching at Providence High's Girl's Department in 1856, and became principal in 1878. Doyle's legacy as a women's rights activist includes cofounding the Rhode Island Women's Club (1876), and playing a key role in the creation of the coed Rhode Island School of Design (1877) and the women's college at Brown University, later named Pembroke College, after its Pembroke Hall, dedicated in 1897. Brown became coed in 1971.

Page 41

"Christian . . . and right living." Quoted in "Matthews, Victoria Earle" by Floris Barnett Cash in Darlene Clark Hine, ed. *Black Women in America: An Historical Encyclopedia.* 2 (Brooklyn: Carlson, 1993), p. 760. **P.S. 83.** The school, located on Schenectady and Bergen streets, had absorbed Colored School No. 68 in the late nineteenth century.

Page 42

Colored School No. 1. Once located on Willoughby Street, the school became P.S. 67 at 51 St. Edwards Street (in the Fort Greene section of Brooklyn) and named the Charles A. Dorsey School.

Page 43

On Maritcha meeting Frederick Douglass. Maritcha provided no date, only indicated that she was a mature woman at the time. Douglass took up residence in Washington, D.C., in 1872 and died in 1895.

Selected Bibliography

Anbinder, Tyler. *Five Points: The 19th-Century New York City Neighborhood that Invented Tap Dance, Stole Elections, and Became the World's Most Notorious Slum*. New York: Plume, 2002.

Bernstein, Ivers. *The New York City Draft Riots: Their Significance for American Society and Politics in the Age of the Civil War*. New York: Oxford University Press, 1990.

Burns, Ric, and James Sanders, with Lisa Ades. *New York: An Illustrated History*. New York: Knopf, 1999.

Burrows, Edwin G., and Mike Wallace. *Gotham: A History of New York City to 1898*. New York: Oxford University Press, 2000.

Dodson, Howard, Christopher Moore, and Roberta Yancey. *The Black New Yorkers: The Schomburg Illustrated Chronology*. New York: John Wiley & Sons, 2000.

Dunshee, Kenneth Holcomb. *As You Pass By: Old Manhattan Through the Fire Laddies' Eyes*. New York: Hastings House, 1952.

Harris, Leslie M. *In the Shadow of Slavery: African Americans in New York City, 1626-1863*. Chicago: University of Chicago Press, 2003.

Harris, M.A. ("Spike"). *A Negro History Tour of Manhattan*. New York: Greenwood Publishing, 1968.

Hodges, Graham Russell. *Root & Branch: African Americans in New York & East Jersey, 1613-1863*. Chapel Hill: University of North Carolina Press, 1999.

Jackson, Kenneth T., ed. *The Encyclopedia of New York City*. New Haven, CT: Yale University Press/The New York Historical Society, 1995.

Johns, Robert L. "Maritcha R. Lyons" in Jessie Carney Smith, ed. *Notable Black American Women: Book II*, pp.: 417-21. Detriot: Gale, 1996.

Johnson, James Weldon. *Black Manhattan* (1930). Reprint with a new introduction by Sondra Kathryn Wilson. New York: Da Capo Press, 1991.

Lyons, Maritcha Rémond. *Memories of Yesterdays: All of Which I Saw and Part of Which I Was* (1928). Harry A. Williamson Papers. New York: The Schomburg Center for Research in Black Culture, The New York Public Library, Astor, Lenox and Tilden Foundations. Sc Micro R-3984, Reel 1.

Rhode Island Black Heritage Society. *Creative Survival: The Providence Black Community in the 19th Century*. Permanent exhibition. Providence, RI.

Tarrant-Reid, Linda. *Discovering Black New York: A Guide to the City's Most Important African American Landmarks, Restaurants, Museums, Historical Sites, and More*. New York: Citadel Press, 2001.

Walker, George. E. *The Afro-American in New York City, 1827-1860*. New York: Garland, 1993.

White, Shane. *Stories of Freedom in Black New York*. Cambridge, MA: Harvard University Press, 2002.

Wilder, Craig Steven. *In the Company of Black Men: The African Influence on African American Culture in New York City*. New York: New York University Press, 2001.

IILLUSTRATION CREDITS

Cover images: (left) Photographs and Prints Division, Schomburg Center for Research in Black Culture, The New York Public Library, Astor, Lenox and Tilden Foundations; [SC-CN-99-194] Nineteenth Century Collection-Ambrotypes. Portrait of Maritcha Lyons and sister, as schoolgirls, ca. 1860 (detail); (top right) Picture Collection, The Branch Libraries, The New York Public Library, Astor, Lenox and Tilden Foundations; [801359] The New York Crystal Palace. [artist: Thomas S. Sinclair]; (bottom right) Eno Collection, Miriam and Ira D. Wallach Division of Art, Prints and Photographs, The New York Public Library, Astor, Lenox and Tilden Foundations; Bachmann, John. *New York and Environs.* 1859. [color lithograph]. Back cover image courtesy of Picture Collection, The Branch Libraries, The New York Public Library, Astor, Lenox and Tilden Foundations; [800182] View of Vandewater St. cor. Frankfort St. (1868). [creator: Major & Knapp Engraving, Manufacturing & Lithographic Co.] **endpapers:** From the author's collection. **Pp. 1, 5:** Photographs and Prints Division, Schomburg Center for Research in Black Culture, The New York Public Library, Astor, Lenox and Tilden Foundations; [SC-CN-99-194] Nineteenth Century Collection-Ambrotypes. Portrait of Maritcha Lyons and sister, as schoolgirls, ca. 1860 (detail). **P. 2:** Manuscripts, Archives & Rare Books Division, Schomburg Center for Research in Black Culture, The New York Public Library, Astor, Lenox and Tilden Foundations; [SC-CN-04-026] Henry Albro Williamson Collection. Title page of *Memories of Yesterdays: All of Which I Saw and Part of Which I Was* by Maritcha Rémond Lyons. **P. 4:** Eno Collection, Miriam and Ira D. Wallach Division of Art, Prints and Photographs, The New York Public Library, Astor, Lenox and Tilden Foundations; Bachmann, John. *New York and Environs.* 1859. [color lithograph]. **P. 6:** Museum of the City of New York; *Five Points*, 1827, Print Archives, 97.227.3. **P. 7:** Manuscripts, Archives & Rare Books Division, Schomburg Center for Research in Black Culture, The New York Public Library, Astor, Lenox and Tilden Foundations; Letterhead and logo of boardinghouse at 880 Pearl Street. **P. 8:** Doll photograph courtesy of Pocumtuck Valley Memorial Association, Memorial Hall Museum, Deerfield, Massachusetts. **P. 9:** North Carolina Museum of Art, Raleigh, Purchased with funds from the State of North Carolina; *Kitchen Ball at White Sulphur Springs, Virginia,* 1838 by Christian Mayr (American, born Germany, about 1805-1851). acct. 52.9.23; CT8683 **P. 10:** Photographs and Prints Division, Schomburg Center for Research in Black Culture, The New York Public Library, Astor, Lenox and Tilden Foundations; Ambrotype of Albert Lyons, Sr., and Mary Lyons (detail). **P. 11:** (Left), Photographs and Prints Division, Schomburg Center for Research in Black Culture, The New York Public Library, Astor, Lenox and Tilden Foundations; Ambrotype of Albert Lyons, Sr., and Mary Lyons (detail). (Top right), Photographs and Prints Division, Schomburg Center for Research in Black Culture, The New York Public Library, Astor, Lenox and Tilden Foundations; [SC-CN-99-194] Nineteenth Century Collection-Ambrotypes. Portrait of Maritcha Lyons and sister, as schoolgirls, ca. 1860 (detail). (Bottom right), Photographs and Prints Division, Schomburg Center for Research in Black Culture, The New York Public Library, Astor, Lenox and Tilden Foundations; Ambrotype of Albro Lyons, Jr., and Mrs. Mary Lyons (detail). **P. 12:** Museum of the City of New York; *American National Game of Base Ball: Grand Match for the Championship at the Elysian Fields, Hoboken, NJ,* 1866, Harry T. Peters Collection, acct. 58.300.34. **P. 13:** (Top), Picture Collection, The Branch Libraries, The New York Public Library, Astor, Lenox and Tilden Foundations; [801359] The New York Crystal Palace. [artist: Thomas S. Sinclair]. (Bottom), Picture Collection, The Branch Libraries, The New York Public Library, Astor, Lenox and Tilden Foundations; [801379] New York Crystal Palace-Interior view no. 2. [artist: Field; engraver; Jocelyn & Annin Whitney]. **P. 15:** Author's collection. **P. 16:** (Top), Engraving of James Hewlett as Kean in Richard III, The Harvard Theater Collection, The Houghton Library. (Bottom), Author's collection. **P. 17:** Collection of the New-York Historical Society, James McCune Smith, bust portrait, engraving by Patrick H. Reason. PR 052 Portrait File. Negative #74638. **P. 18:** Photographs and Prints Division, Schomburg Center for Research in Black Culture, The New York Public Library, Astor, Lenox and Tilden Foundations; [SC-CN-97-0178] *Harper's Weekly.* February 26, 1870. "Colored School-Object Teaching." African Free School, New York City. **P. 19:** Eno Collection, Miriam and Ira D. Wallach Division of Art, Prints and Photographs, The New York Public Library, Astor, Lenox and Tilden Foundations; Girardet, Paul, after Sebron, Hippolyte V. V. *Winter Scene on Broadway.* 1857. [color aquatint with additional hand-coloring]. **P. 20:** Photographs and Prints Division, Schomburg Center for Research in Black Culture, The New York Public Library, Astor, Lenox and Tilden Foundations; [SC-CN-95-0453] *Harper's Weekly.* April 9, 1864. Page 237. "Negroes Leaving Their Home." **P. 21:** Author's collection. **P. 23:** Picture Collection, The Branch Libraries, The New York Public Library, Astor, Lenox and Tilden Foundations; [800182] View of Vandewater St. cor. Frankfort St. (1868). [creator: Major & Knapp Engraving, Manufacturing & Lithographic Co.]. **P. 25:** Picture Collection, The Branch Libraries, The New York Public Library, Astor, Lenox and Tilden Foundations; [809566] New York-burning of the provost marshal's office. [188?]. **P. 26:** (Top) Collection of the New-York Historical Society, Sacking Brooks Department Store, The Riots at New York, July 1868. Negative #43199. (Bottom) Collection of the New-York Historical Society, Rioters Chasing Negro Women and Children, NYC Draft Riots, 1863. Negative #40828. **P. 27:** Author's collection. **P. 29:** Picture Collection, The Branch Libraries, The New York Public Library, Astor, Lenox and Tilden Foundations; [809560] *Battle of the barricades.* 1887. [artist: Tresch]. **P. 30:** Manuscripts, Archives & Rare Books Division, Schomburg Center for Research in Black Culture, The New York Public Library, Astor, Lenox and Tilden Foundations; First page of inventory of Lyons' loss during draft riots. **P. 31:** *American Express Train,* 1864, published by Currier & Ives, hand-colored lithograph, Museum of the City of New York, Harry T. Peters Collection acct. 56.300.103. **P. 32:** Author's collection. **P. 33:** Author's collection. **P. 34:** Manuscripts, Archives & Rare Books Division, Schomburg Center for Research in Black Culture, The New York Public Library, Astor, Lenox and Tilden Foundations; Henry A. Williamson Collection. Flyer for Lyons' Ice Cream Depot. **P. 35:** Cover and detail from page 225 of *Acts and Resolves Passed at the January Session of the General Assembly of the State of Rhode Island and Providence Plantations, 1866.* Courtesy of Special Collections, University of Rhode Island. **P. 37:** Rhode Island Collection at Providence Public Library; photo of Providence High. **P. 38:** (Left), Manuscripts, Archives & Rare Books Division, Schomburg Center for Research in Black Culture, The New York Public Library, Astor, Lenox and Tilden Foundations; Cover page of Maritcha Lyons' high school graduation speech. (Right), Manuscripts, Archives & Rare Books Division, Schomburg Center for Research in Black Culture, The New York Public Library, Astor, Lenox and Tilden Foundations; First page of Maritcha Lyons' high school graduation speech. **P. 40:** Photographs and Prints Division, Schomburg Center for Research in Black Culture, The New York Public Library, Astor, Lenox and Tilden Foundations; Portrait of middle-aged Maritcha Lyons. **P. 42:** Ohio Historical Society; cover of *Homespun Heroines.* Call no. 920.073.B818h.

TEXT CREDITS

For permission to quote from Maritcha Lyons's memoir *Memories of Yesterdays: All of Which I Saw, Some of Which I Was*; Maritcha Lyons's high school graduation essay; Albro Lyons's "*Inventory*" of losses during the July 1868 Draft Riots; The Lyons Family Genealogical Records; and the January 1896 *New York Age* article "*Death of Albro Lyons,*" grateful acknowledgment is made to the Harry A. Williamson Papers, Manuscripts, Archives and Rare Books Division, Schomburg Center for Research in Black Culture, The New York Public Library, Astor, Lenox and Tilden Foundations.

ACKNOWLEDGMENTS

What a glory to do another book with such a terrific editor as Howard Reeves, his snappy assistant Linas Alsenas, and the eagle-eyed production editor Andrea Colvin. How wonderful to have the benefit of the deft designing minds of Becky Terhune and Ed Miller. Thanks also to Abrams' Jason Wells and Nicholas Gaudiuso for their post-production work.

I truly would not have been able to do this book without the cooperation and tremendous assistance of The New York Public Library's Schomburg Center for Research in Black Culture. I thank the Schomburg's chief, Howard Dodson, for his support and encouragement over the years. In Prints & Photographs, bless you Mary Yearwood, division curator; Antony M. Toussaint, Linden Anderson, Jr., and Michael Mery. In Manuscripts, Archives, and Rare Books--André Elizée, with everlasting gratitude to division curator, Diana Lachatanere, the good soul who introduced me to Maritcha's memoir. For research rescue, thanks is also due to the Schomburg's Sharon Howard, Christopher Moore, and Alice Adamczyk. Tom Lisanti, manager of The New York Public Library's Photographic Services & Permissions--you are such a pleasure to deal with, such a gem.

From fact-finding to finding artwork, I was fortunate to encounter gems at other institutions as well. Thank you so much assistant professor Sarina Rodrigues Wyant, assistant archivist, Special Collections librarian at the University of Rhode Island; Kenneth R. Cobb, director of the Municipal Archives, City of New York Department of Records and Information Services; Robert A. McInnes, site administrator and archivist for the New London County Historical Society; Melanie Bower, collections access assistant, and Faye Haun, Rights & Reproductions associate, at the Museum of the City of New York; Marybeth Kavanagh, director of Rights & Reproductions at the New-York Historical Society; Marcia Erickson, registrar at the North Carolina Museum of Art; Louise Jones in Research Services and Duryea Kemp in the Archives-Library division of the Ohio Historical Society; Fredric Woodbridge Wilson, curator, Kathleen Coleman, curatorial assistant, and Lucas Dennis, reference and public services Assistant, at the Houghton Library's Harvard Theatre Collection; Greg Frazier and Joe Rawson in Reference Services and Elizabeth Fitzgerald with Rhode Island Collection of the Providence Public Library; Jacqueline Alves with the Providence Public School System; Christine Granat, curatorial assistant at the Pocumtuck Valley Memorial Association; and Bela Teixeira, executive director of the Rhode Island Black Heritage Society. I also thank Kevin McGruder for help with research and factchecking; scholar on black New York Craig Steven Wilder for responding to queries; and Susan Hess, library media specialist at Brooklyn's Juan Morel Campos Intermediate School 71, and Nelta Brunson Gallemore (my sister) for their feedback on early drafts of the manuscript.

For all these people and this book, I thank the Almighty.

Designed by Edward Miller
Production Manager: Jonathan Lopes

The Library of Congress has catalogued the hardcover edition of this book as follows:

Bolden, Tonya.
Maritcha : a nineteenth-century American girl / Tonya Bolden.
p. cm.
ISBN 978-0-8109-5045-0
1. Lyons, Maritcha Rémond, 1848-1929--Juvenile literature. 2. African American girls--New York (State--New York--Biography--Juvenile literature. 3. Free African Americans--New York (State)--New York--Biography--Juvenile literature. 4. African Americans--New York (State)--New York--Social life and customs--19th century--Juvenile literature. 5. New York (State)--Social life and customs--19th century--Juvenile literature. 6. New York (State)--Social conditions--19th century--Juvenile literature. 7. New York (State)--Race relations--Juvenile literature. I. Title.

F128.9.N4B65 2004
974.71'00496073--dc22
2004005849

ISBN for this edition: 978-1-4197-1626-3

Text copyright © 2005 Tonya Bolden
Copyright © 2005 Harry N. Abrams, Inc.
For illustration credits, see page 47.

Printed and bound in China
10 9 8 7 6 5 4 3 2

ABRAMS
THE ART OF BOOKS SINCE 1949
115 West 18th Street
New York, NY 10011
www.abramsbooks.com

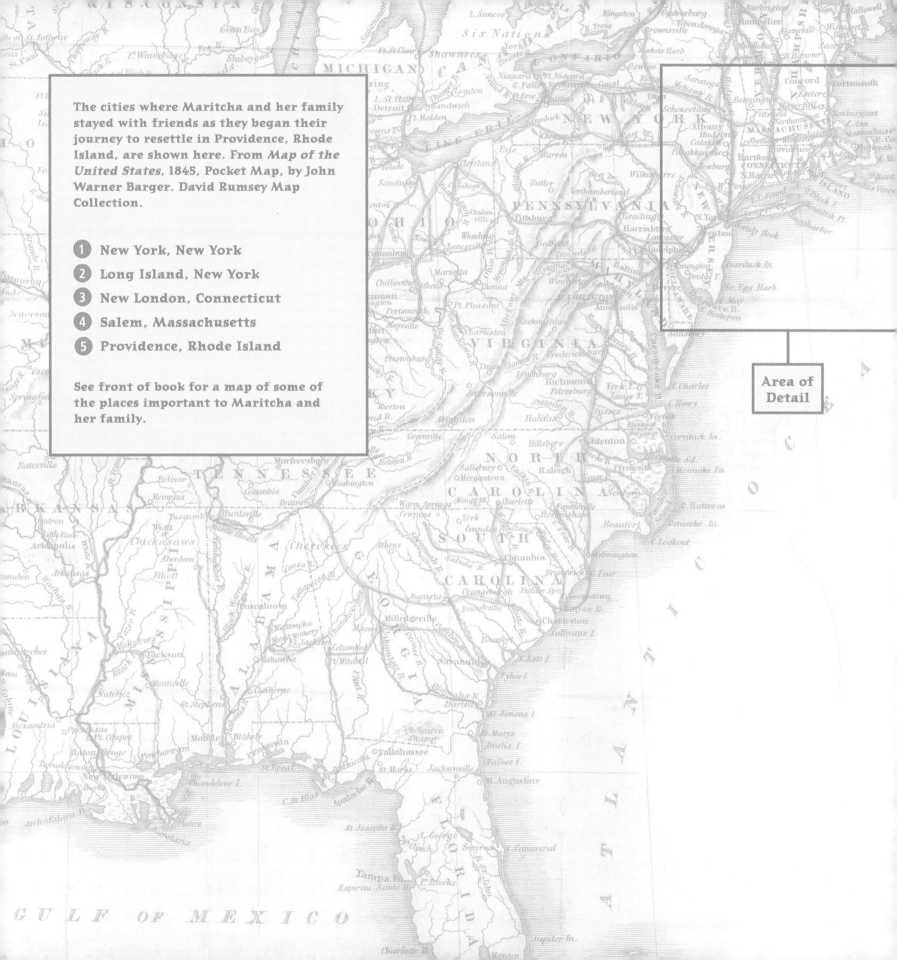

The cities where Maritcha and her family stayed with friends as they began their journey to resettle in Providence, Rhode Island, are shown here. From *Map of the United States*, 1845, Pocket Map, by John Warner Barger. David Rumsey Map Collection.

1 New York, New York

2 Long Island, New York

3 New London, Connecticut

4 Salem, Massachusetts

5 Providence, Rhode Island

See front of book for a map of some of the places important to Maritcha and her family.

Area of Detail